~A Walk-About~

The Capitol

Black & White

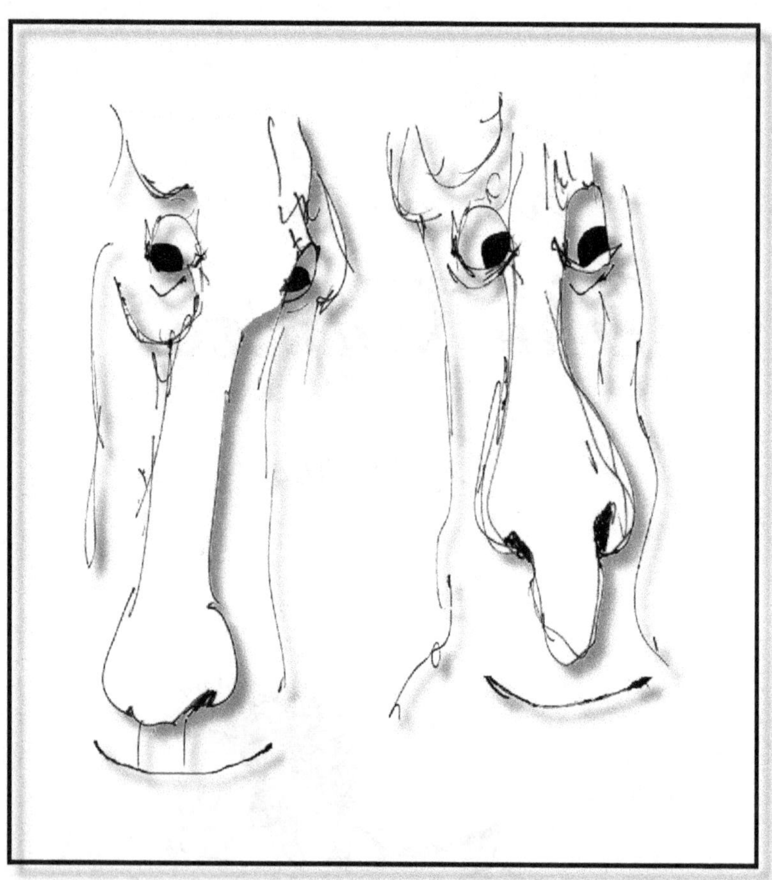

A Seek-and-Find Adventure Book

A-Walk-About

The Capitol

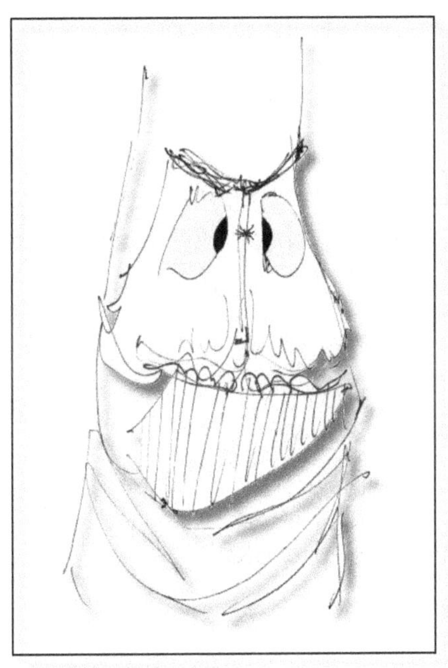

~ Introducing ~

The Honorable

Senator Gospelle

To a Rose

The stories in this book are meant as humorous tales only. They are designed to be entertaining but thought provoking. Use your own imagination and see what other friendly creatures you can find around Capitol Park. (But don't blame me if they scare you.)

The world of Pareidolia – a world where you see images, faces and shapes in random or vague visual patterns in the things around you.

A Seek-and-Find Adventure Book

A~Walk~About The Capitol B&W

ISBN 9781973739401
Library of Congress number 2017940582

The Bartolimus Bros.
~ Cedo and Bedo ~

These two brothers are the unofficial - official greeters to Capitol Park. They are always in such a good mood; even in the spring, when the wind is blowing and the pollen count is so high that Bees don't dare fly. They have said, "Hello, Good-By, 'How-Are-You', 'Have-A-Nice-Day', and 'Please speak up. I've got really bad allergies today," more than 12 million 300 and 23 thousand times so far. But they're not counting.

So drop by and say 'Hi' to them, won't you? But, if you're there in the Spring, they may ask you to stand back when they blow their noses.

11

Captain Jackson

Captain Jackson is the head of security for the entire Capitol Park, but he doesn't want to see your I.D. or your clearance badge or your security card or even your driver's license. He just wants to check your palms.

<u>10</u>

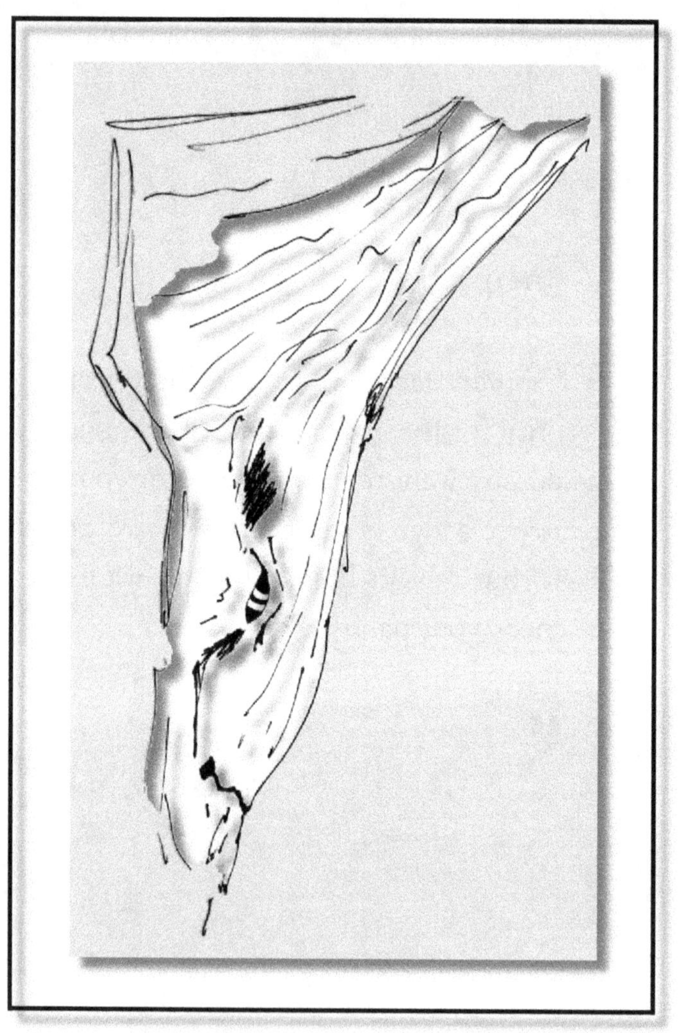

Chief Justice Kronox

Chief Justice Kronox is the Supreme Justice of The California Trees. His job is to hear arguments and complaints presented by The Lower Courts of Trees. He has a talent for getting to the root of any problem and providing rulings that are fair and just to all trees.

But at the end of a session, his favorite thing to do is to order for some Rocky Road and Mint Chip fertilizer for the entire court, including his great great great uncle "General Sherman", a giant Sequoia tree in Sequoia National Park said to be 2,200 years old, but that was several years ago.

20

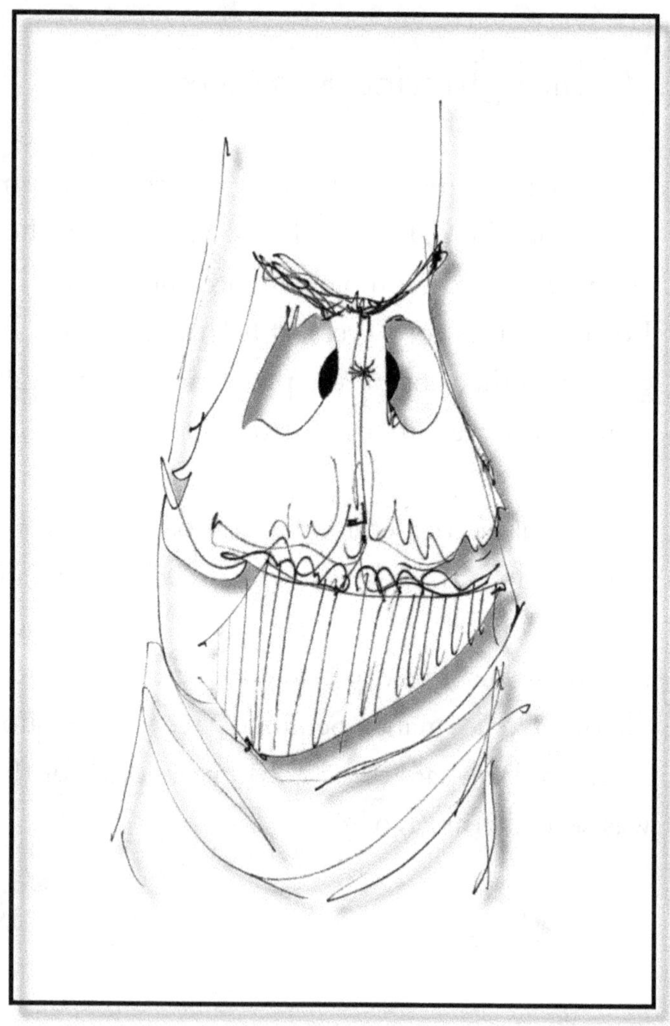

Senator "Gabby" Gospelle

Senator Gospelle loves to talk and talk and talk, and will talk to anybody, any time, about anything and everything. On this day he was busy talking endlessly to a spider about *who had invented dirt* and *why had they made so much of it . . . (The spider fell asleep.)*

20

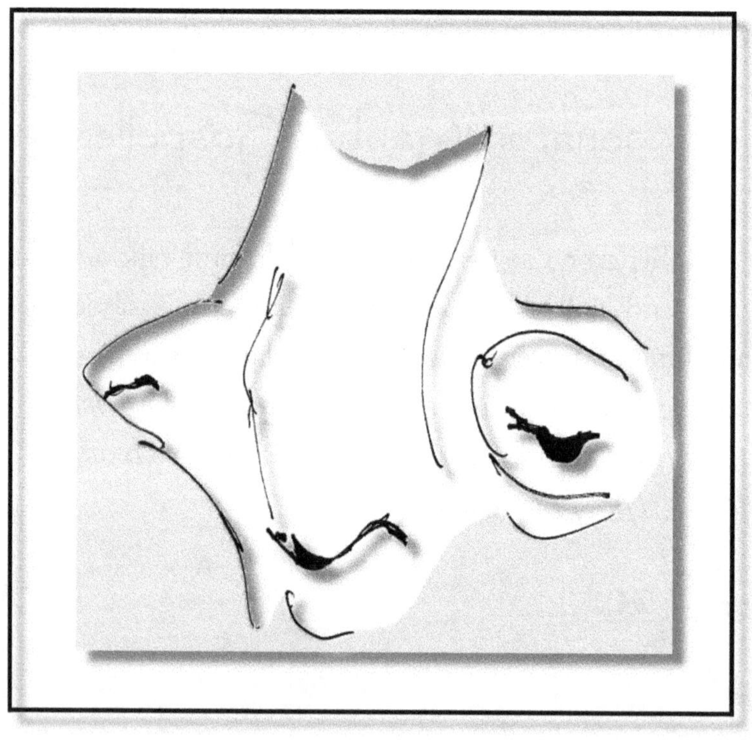

Grip-Slaugh
(The Tree Glyph)

Grip-Slaugh is a Tree Glyph. It is a good sign to find a Tree Glyph because they only live in happy and healthy forests and parks. Whenever you see a Tree Glyph you know that the trees are being cared for properly. But don't get too close to a Tree Glyph, they can drool SAP on you.

7

The Tree of Wisdom
And the Node of Knowledge

It is said that if you rest against this magnificent tree and put your hand on its huge friendly looking node while thinking over a difficult problem, you will receive a valuable answer. *(It worked for me)*

The NODE is a People Whisperer, so listen very carefully.

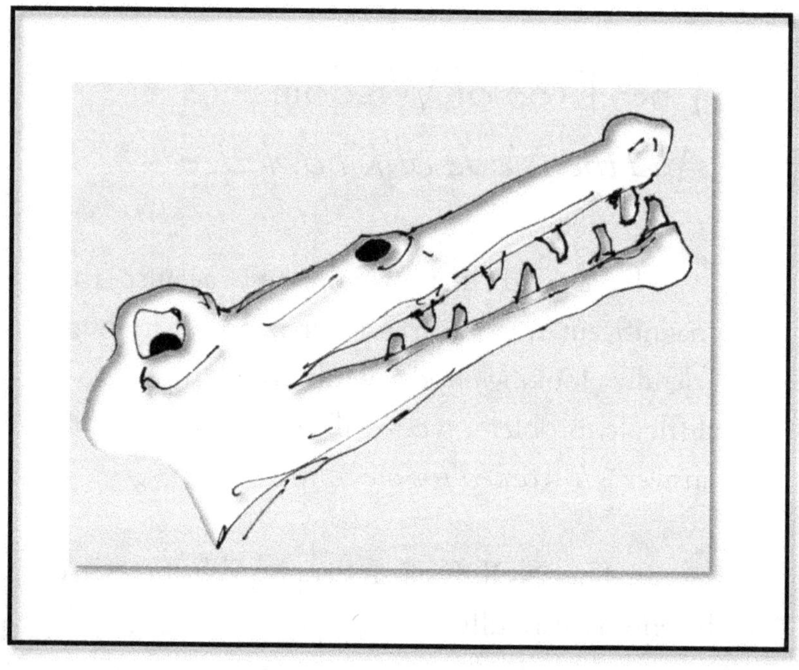

The Alligator Tree

The Alligator is the spirit of endurance and perseverance and is a strong connection to Mother Earth. Its spirit is said to be the protector of all knowledge. When you encounter the spirit of the Alligator you will soon learn something new that will gain you wisdom.

<u>15</u>

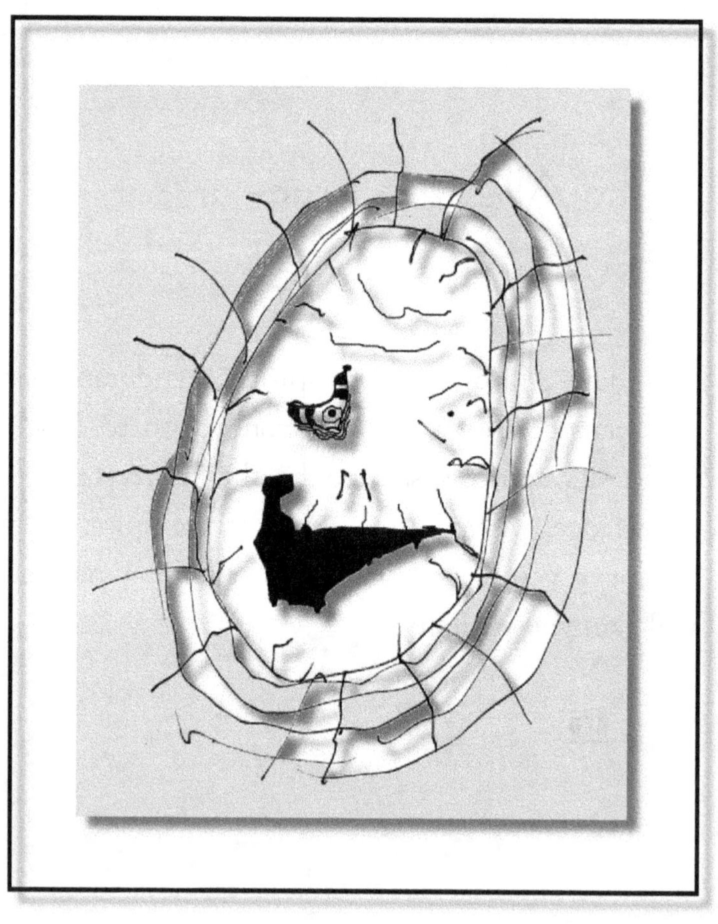

Tommie the Black-eyed Zombie

If you happen to see Tommie during the day, be very quiet because he's probably sleeping. One day, at around 2 Oh! Clock, Tommie scared a group from France. One lady was so frightened that she hit Tommie with her purse, right in the eye, and knocked 3 teeth out. Tommie now only comes out at night to do his scaring, but he always makes sure no one is around … he doesn't want to lose any more teeth.

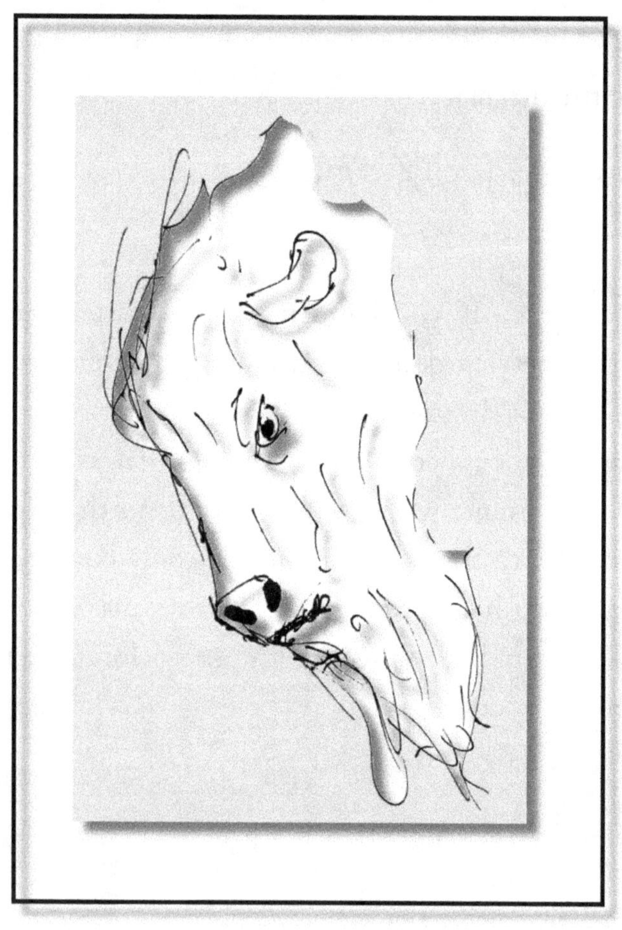

The Buffalo Tree

The Buffalo is one of the strongest animal spirits you will find. The spirit of the Buffalo teaches that when you are grateful for what you have and live in balance with all things around you, you will have harmony. The Buffalo's energy will also help you find hidden talents and abilities within yourself.

19

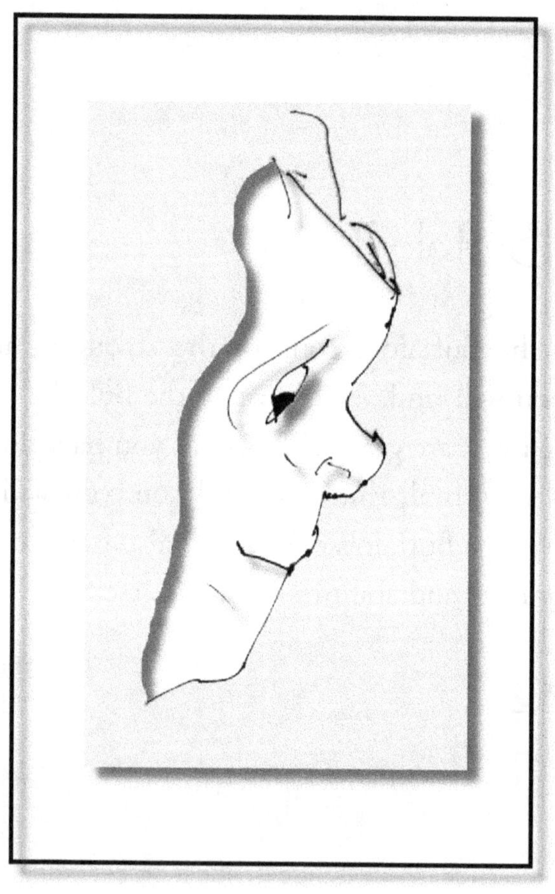

The Quiet Man

The Quiet Man is a gentle and kind tree spirit who will listen to whatever you have to say. He loves to hear your opinions on anything and will listen to you as long as you want to talk. He is the best listener in Capitol Park and says, "Sometimes, it's best to just listen and let people hear their own words. That's the best way to find a worthy solution."

12

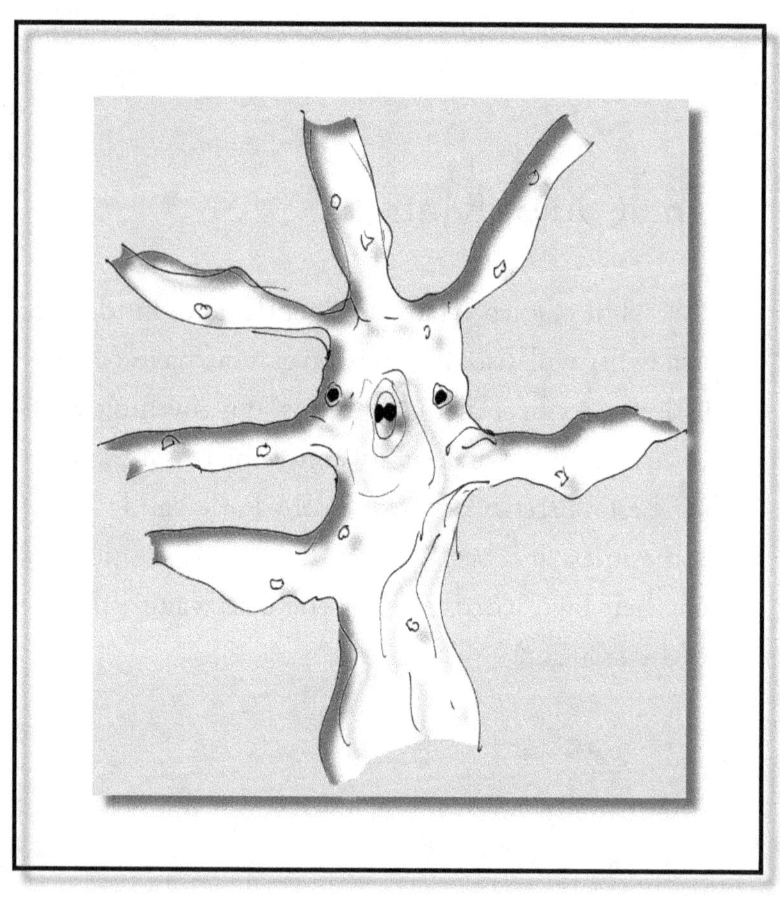

The Octopus Tree

The Octopus is the spirit of flexibility, creativity and determination. The Octopus' spirit will show you imaginative alternatives and creative ways to obtain the goals you have set for yourself and it will strengthen your determination to accomplish them.

<u>18</u>

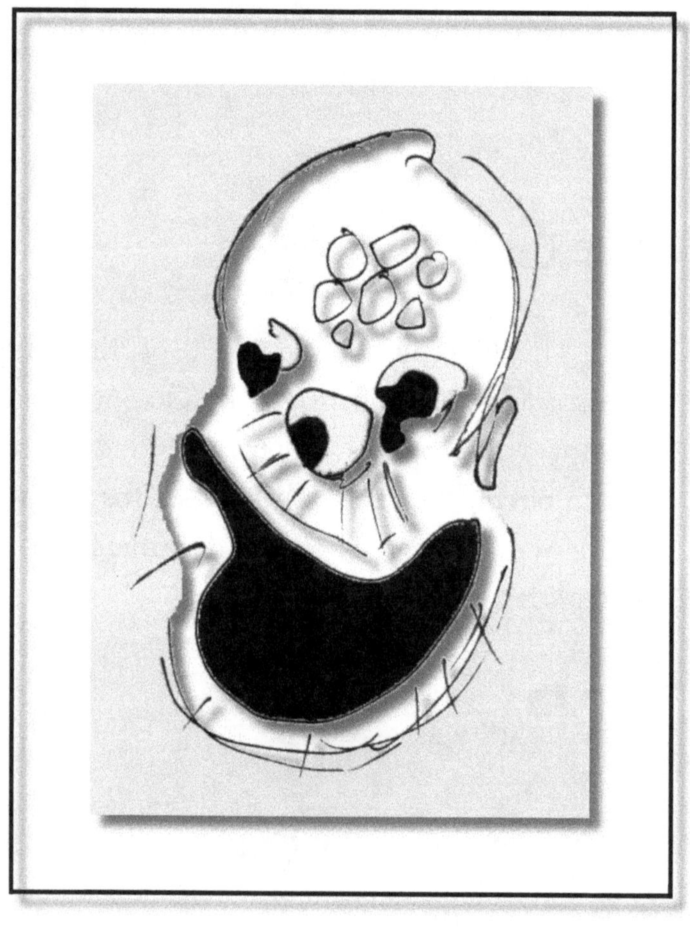

Sappy the Tree Clown

This is Sappy the Tree Clown. He came to California's 100th birthday celebration on September 9th, 1950 and never left. He is still having such a good time that no one has the heart to tell him that the party's been over for more than 60 years. If you happen to pass by him he may want you to sing "Happy Birthday" with him. *(Just play along)*

14

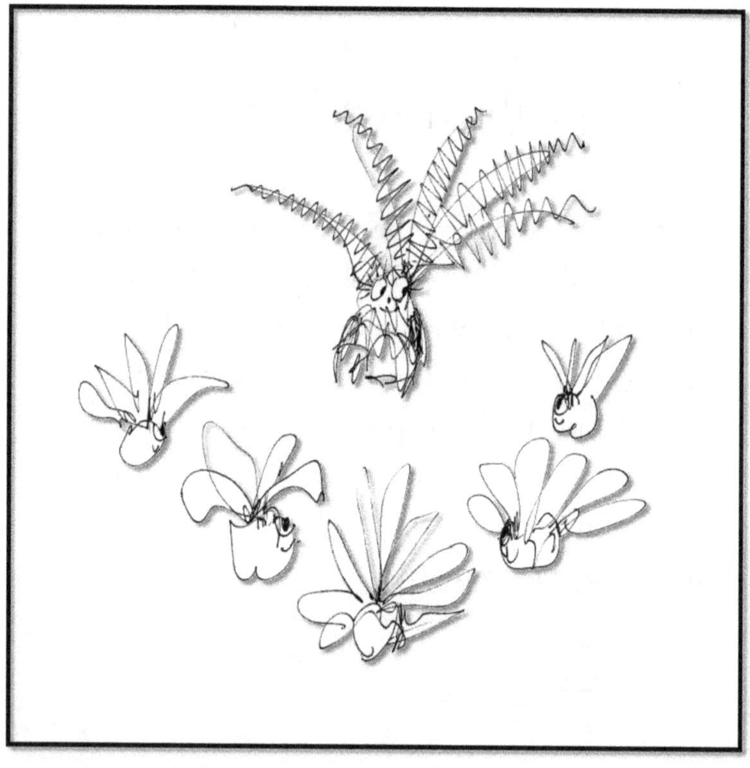

Mrs. Steel's 1st Grade Class

Mrs. Steel just loves to teach her class about Government. She explains that it is the Government that makes the laws we live by which helps us play fair and treat each other with respect. And it's the Government that collects the taxes to pay for all the Policemen, Firemen and Gardeners to do their jobs properly. But, usually, all the little plants want to know is, *"Where do seeds come from?"*

22

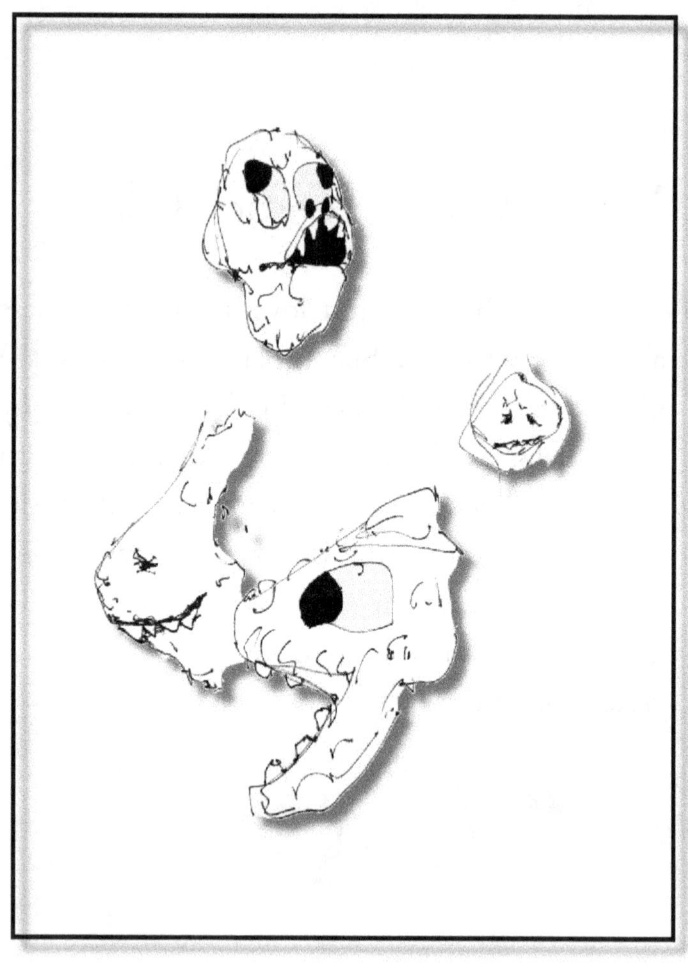

The Wickeds

The Wickeds scare away any bad thoughts or ideas that might be entering the Park. They protect the good spirits of the trees so that they may enjoy their life in the Park, and yes, this even includes Tommie, the Black-Eyed Zombie. If you are having a bad day, just go near the Wickeds and your day's fortunes will most likely change.

<u>13</u>

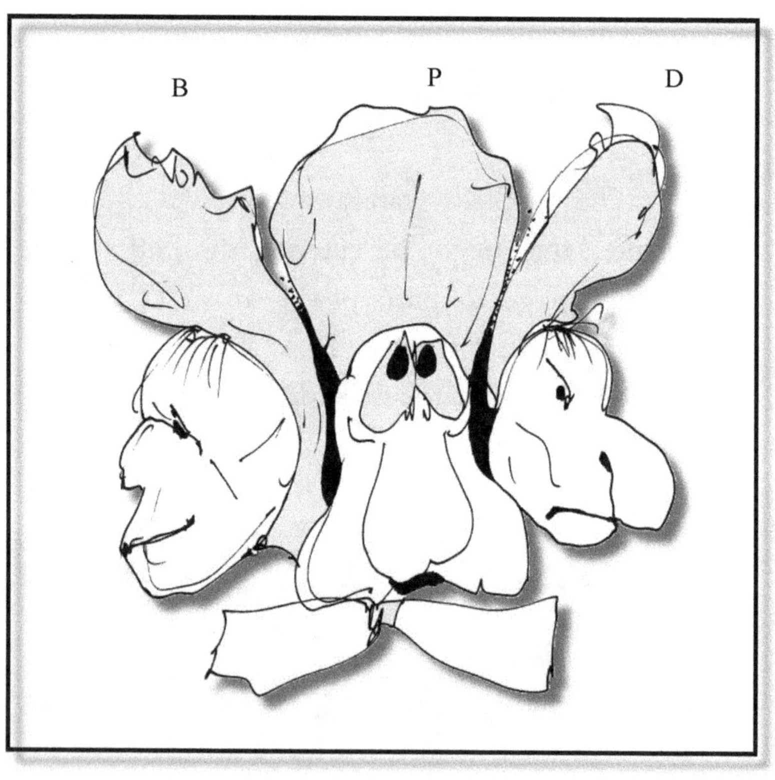

B
P
D

Budzey, Ploom and Dumo

These three chaps attend every function at the State Capitol, but they are definitely an odd trio of sorts. Budzey always has a good time no matter what happens, Dumo complains about everything no matter how much fun he is having, and Ploom always forgets to bring the tickets, AND bug spray.

2

The Owl Man

The Owl Man is a Super Hero by day and a Super Spy by night. He catches villains by the thousands each year and has received hundreds of medals and awards. But his only complaint is that his Mom makes him wash his hands and change his underwear every time he changes from his Hero Uniform to his Spy Uniform.

17

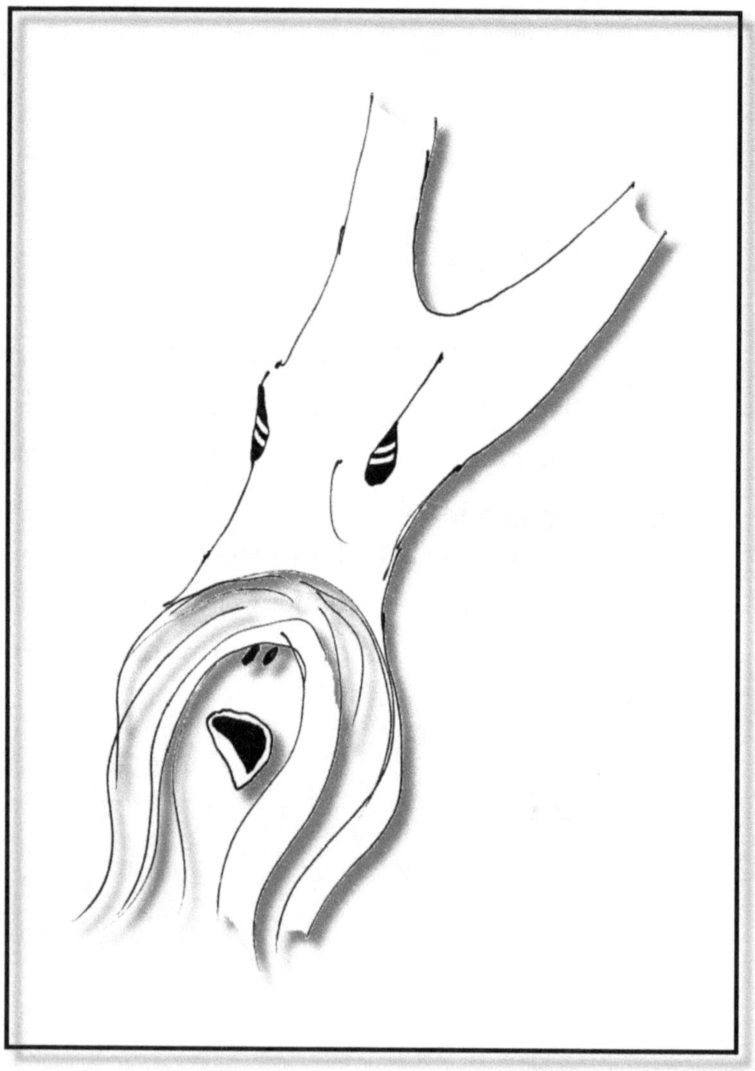

Senator Orzlock

Senator Orzlock is the Speaker of The House of Trees and is a very well respected and honored member of the Senate. He also lectures at the State's Deciduous Universities and reads poetry to all the young buds and blossoms throughout the Park. His nick name is 'Grandpa Whispering Whiskers'.

3

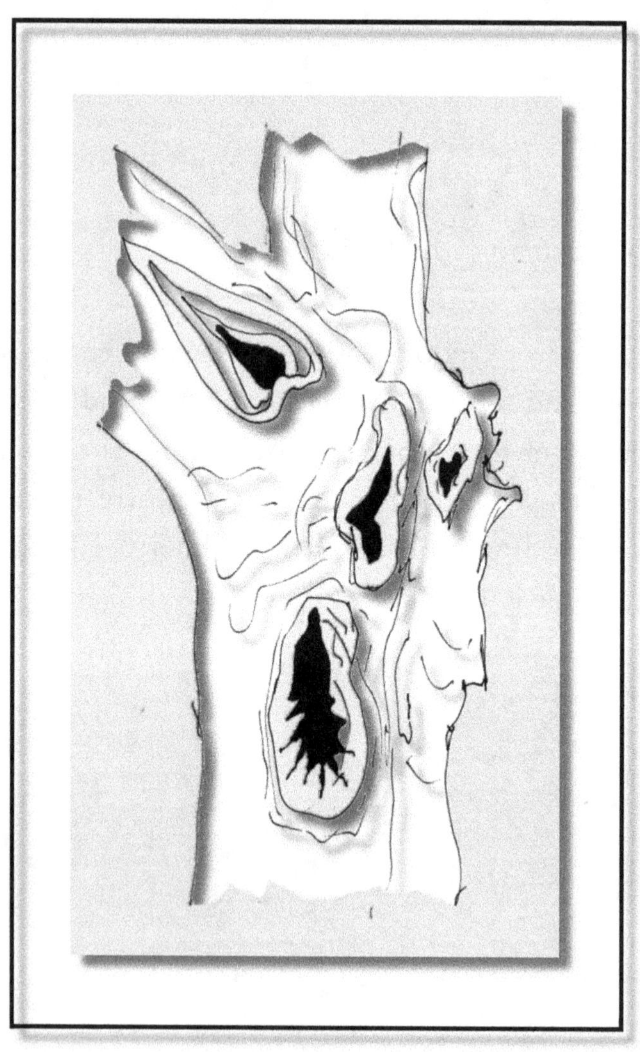

McKhoul the Ghoul

McKhoul the Ghoul used to be called McKhoul the Cool until the day when he made some scary bizarre faces at some visiting dignitaries from the Tongass National Forest in Alaska, and his bark froze that way. The moral of this story is: "Be careful what you do because you may have to live with what you have done ... for the rest of your life."

<u>16</u>

Professor JuNo

The professor's watching
From way up high,
To see if you,
Or even I,
Have learned a thing
About these trees,
And if we have,
Then he is pleased.

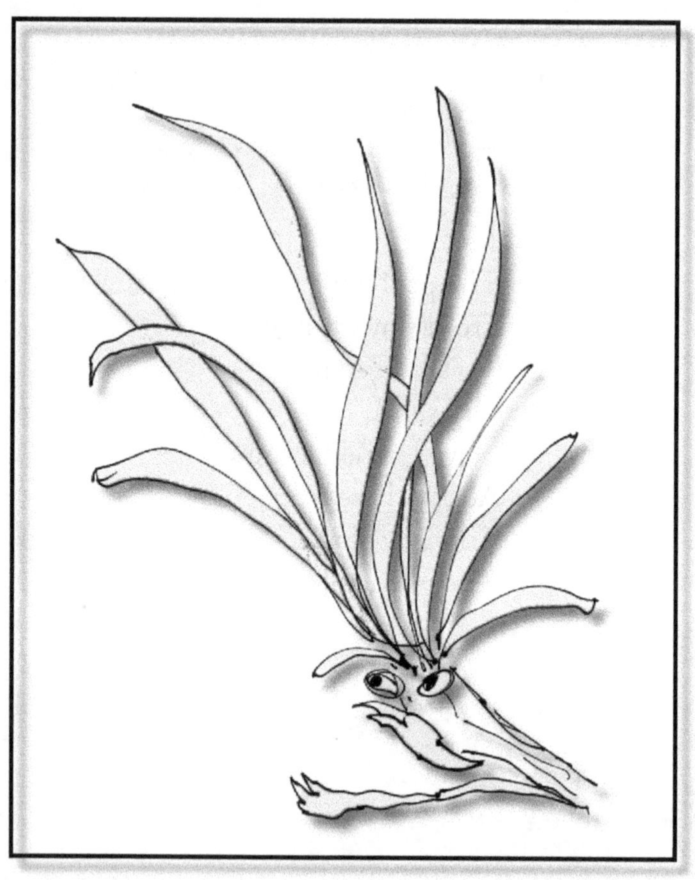

Ace Stonebox

Ace Stonebox loves to tell stories about the Flying Insect Aces and their magnificent aerial combat maneuvers. Why, just the other day he was telling a story about how Maxi Mosquito did a midair flip, three twists while diving and ended up biting a lobbyist from L.A.; once on the end of his nose, twice behind his ear and three times where he sits down.

24

Madam Boshay

Madam Boshay is the Primo-Lady of Capitol Park and the special events organizer. She arranges all the parties, prepares all the schedules, arranges for all the entertainment and orders all the food. She never settles for anything but the highest quality fertilizers, which come from…well, she's not saying, but you can bet it's the best from all around. Just smell it, it's P-U-tiful. BUT, you must put in your request no later than the beginning of Spring.

1

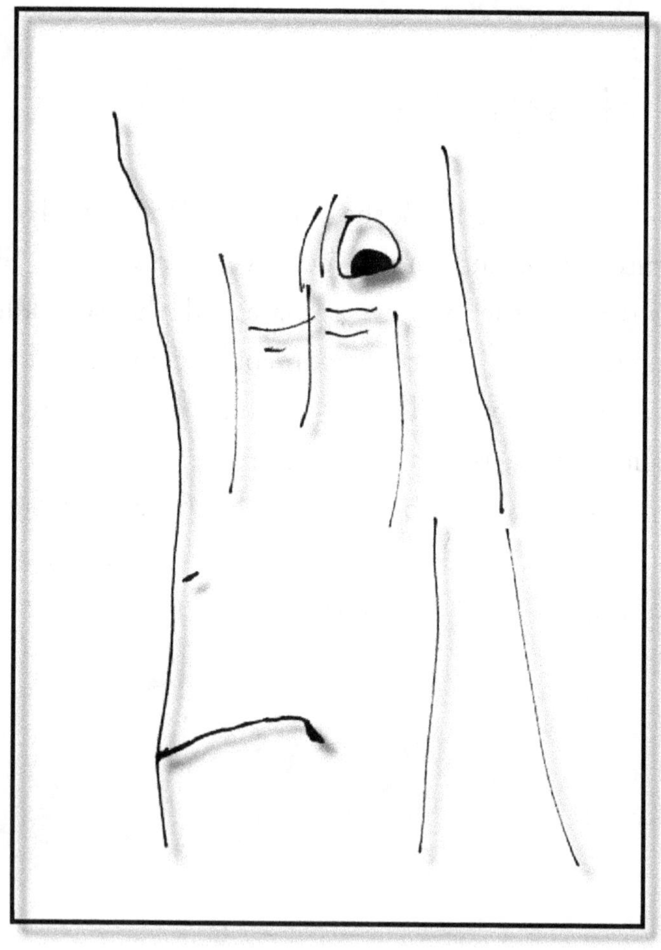

Senator Goodspell

Senator Goodspell is the official Bill Writer for the Tree Senate. A Bill is the written description of a law someone wants to pass. The Bill is presented to the Tree Senate for a vote and if it passes, the Bill then becomes a Law. He's busy now writing a Bill that would make it illegal to have a bad day.

4

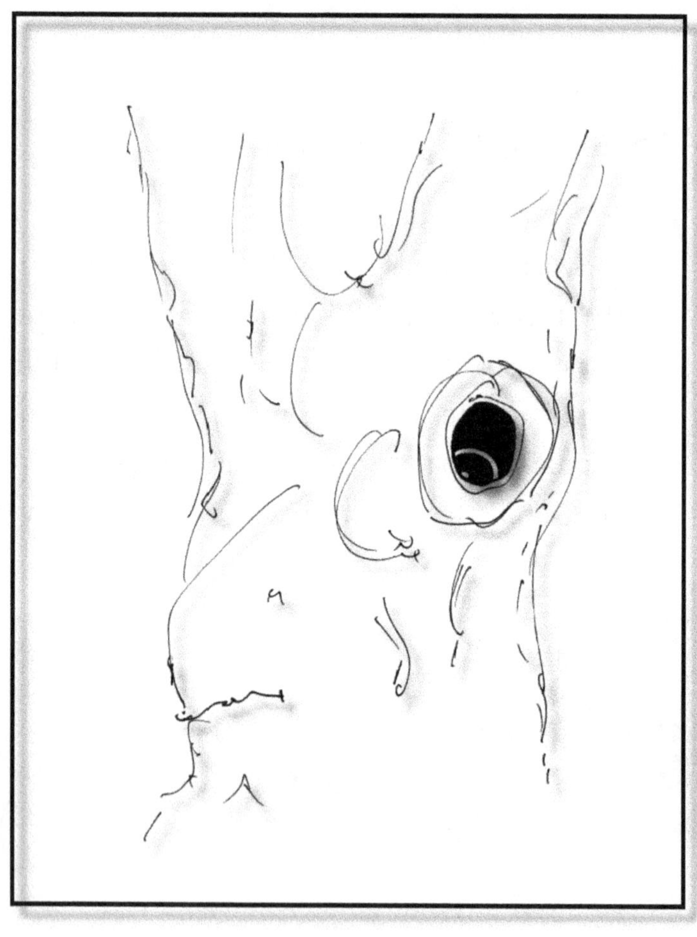

The Amunggus

The Amunggus is for lovers. With his deep watchful eye he can look into your heart and see if true love is near. The look of love is always undeniable and he can always tell if two people are in love. He will spread the word to every tree in the Park and wherever you go the trees will know. He will also notify the wind so you don't have to.

22

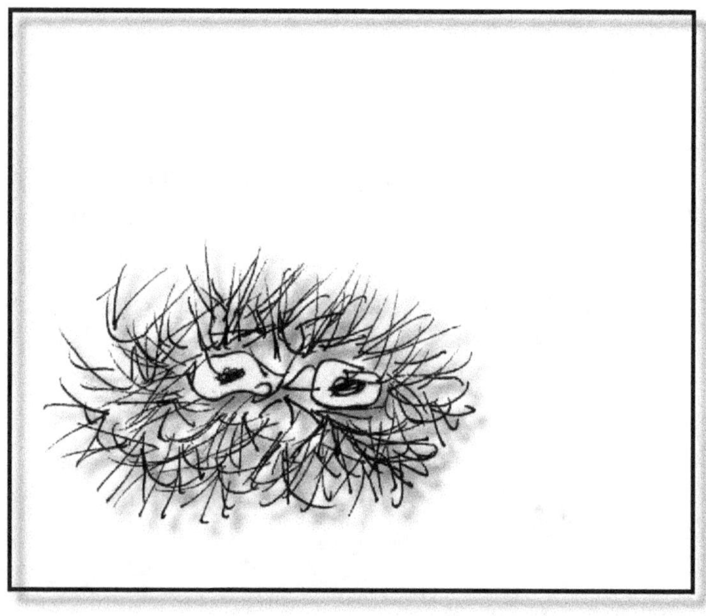

The Fuzz-What

The Fuzz-What is a clump, and he has many sisters and brothers. No telling where he will show up but you can be certain he's at every event in the Park. He has many many friends. There is no picture of Fuzz-What cuz he's everywhere you look.

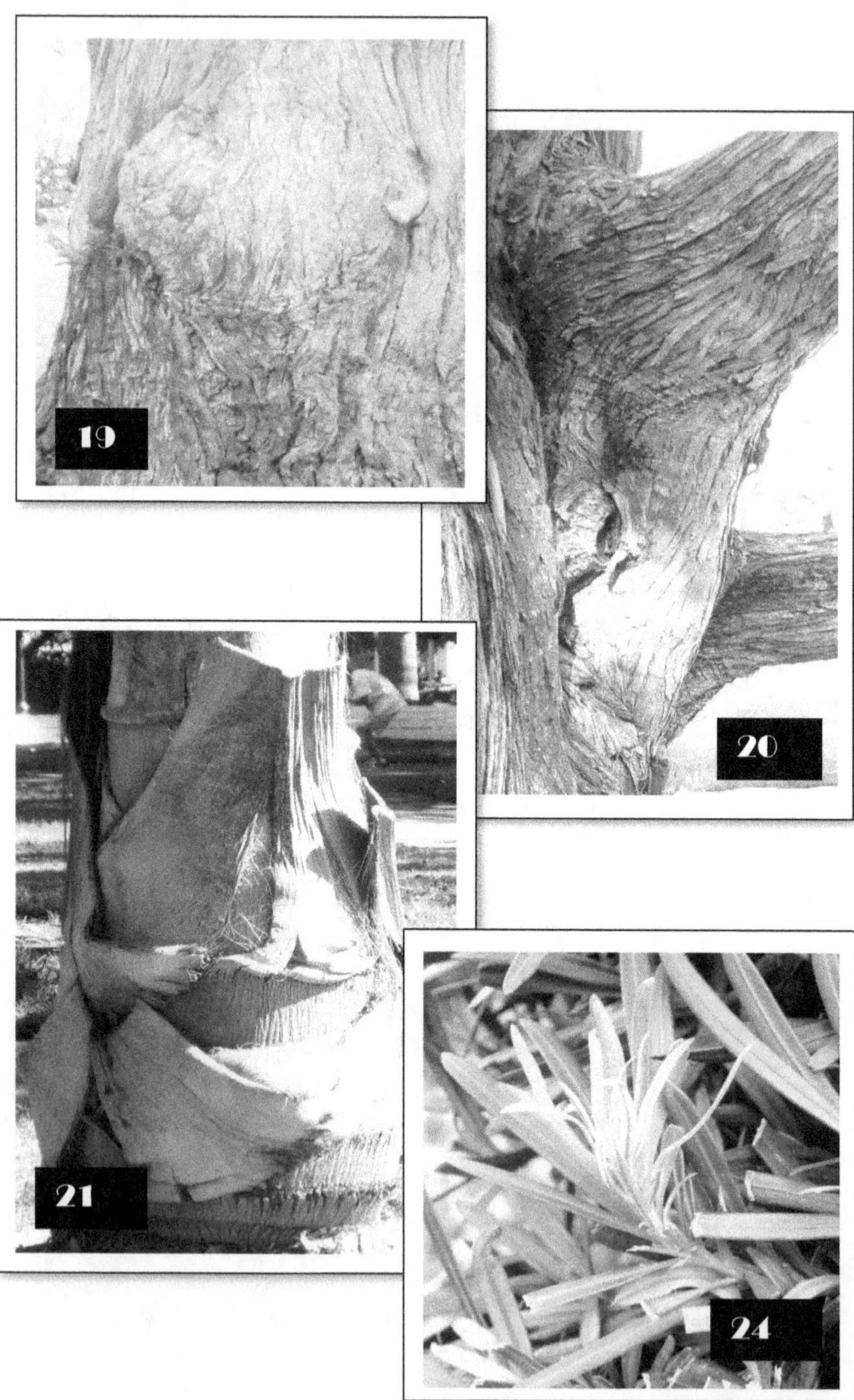

5
4
6
1

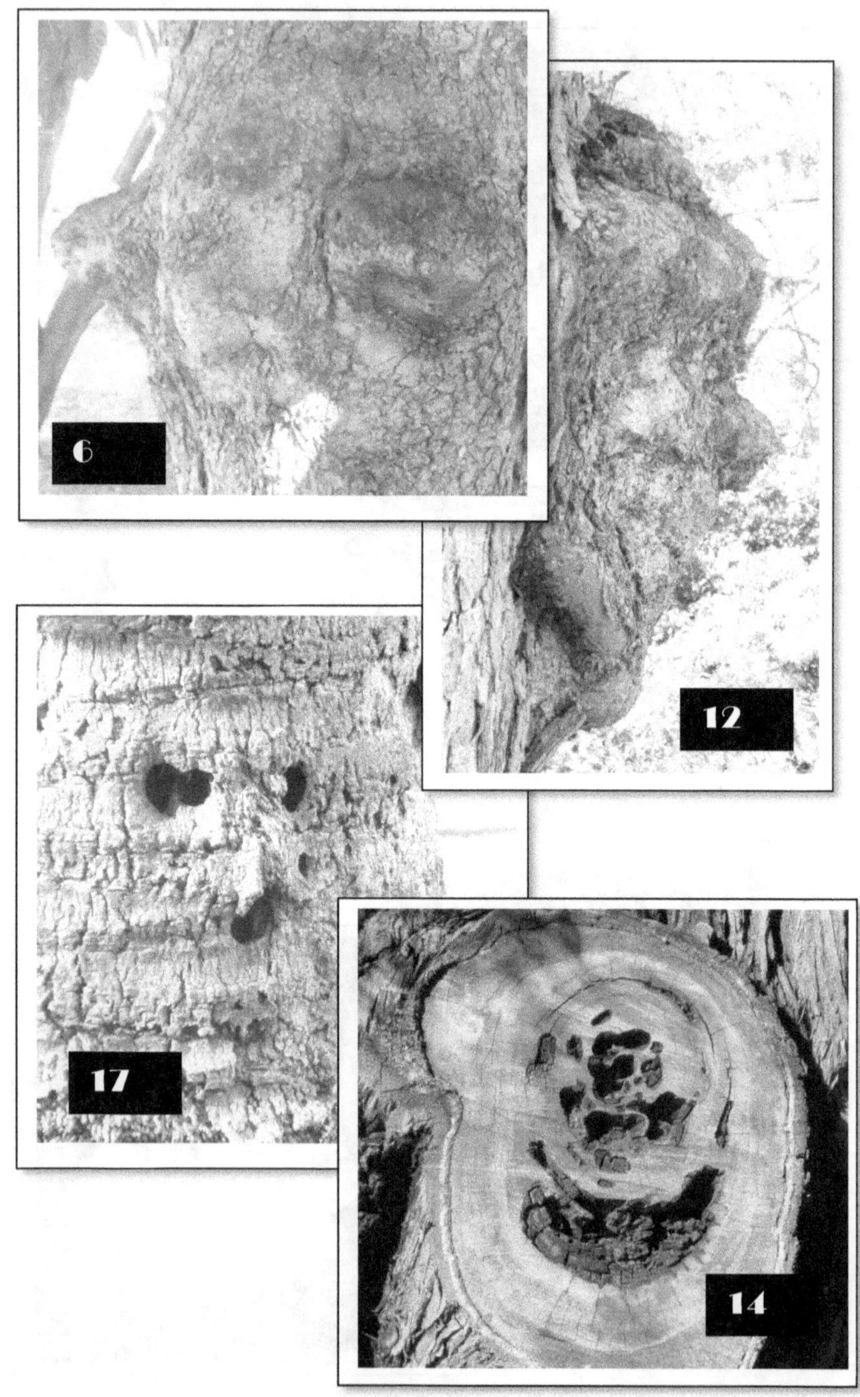

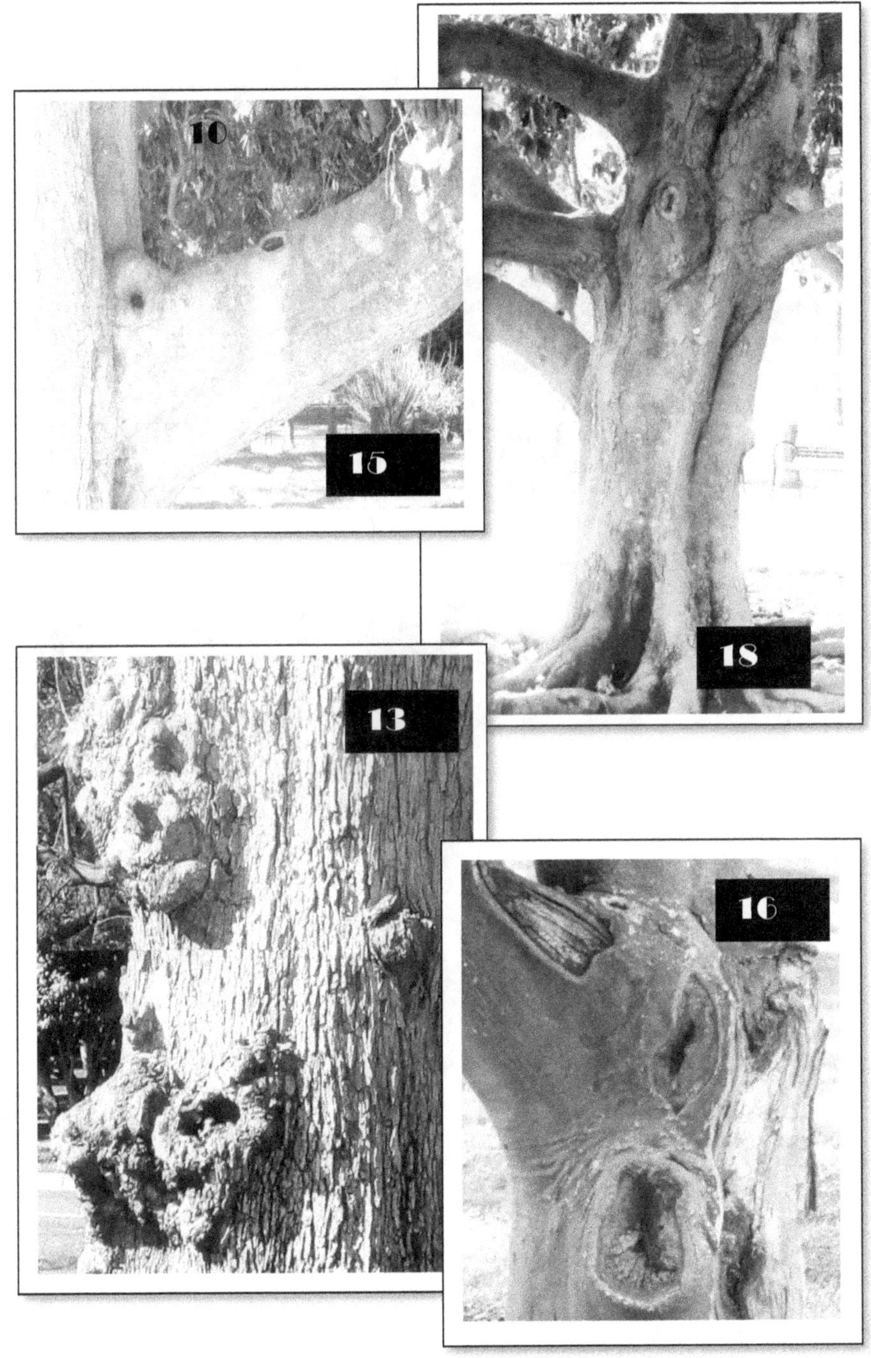

10
15
18
13
16

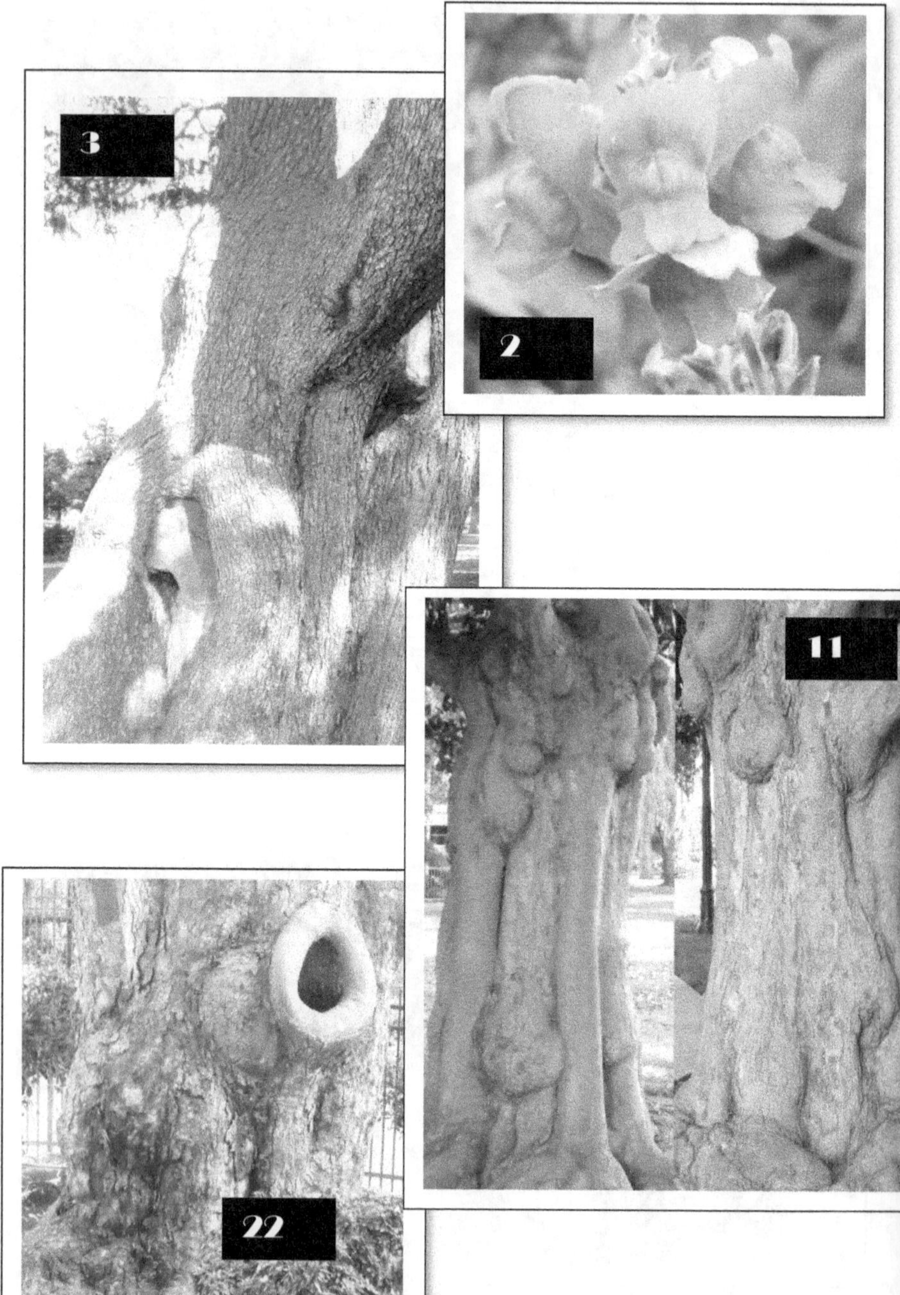

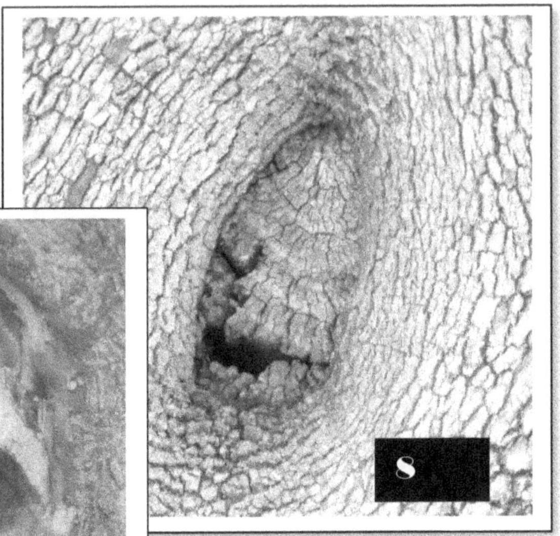

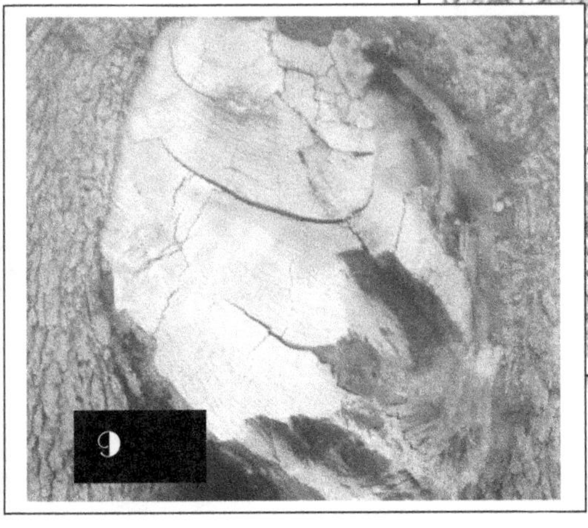

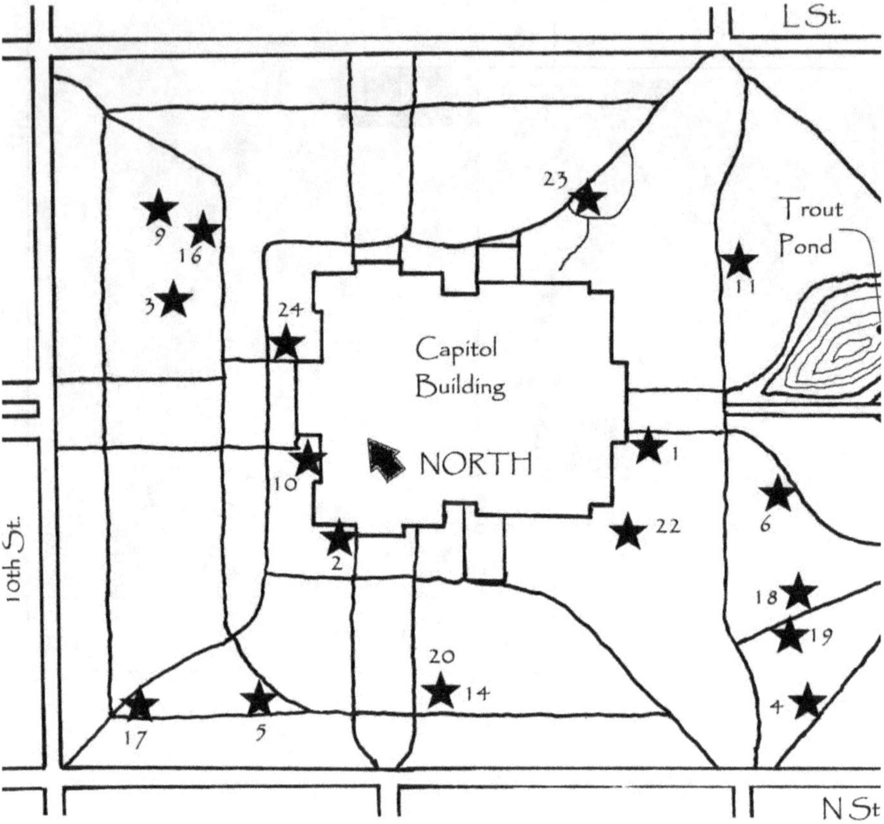

1. Madam Boshay
2. Budzey, Ploom & Dumo
3. Senator Orzlock
4. Senator Goodspell
5. The Tree of Wisdom &
    The Node of Knowledge
6. Professor JuNo
7. The Grip Slaugh
8. Tommie the Black-eyed
    Zombie
9. The Eagle Tree
10. Captain Jackson
11. The Bartolimus Bros.
    Cedo & Bedo

Discovery Map

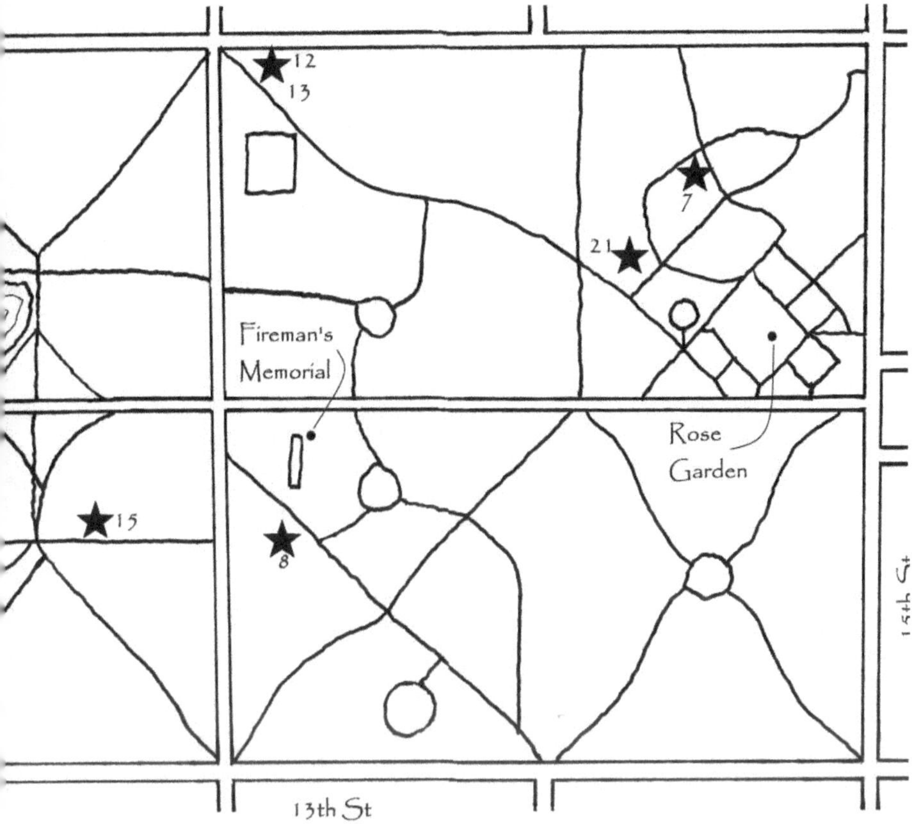

12. The Quiet Man
13. The Wickeds
14. Sappy the Tree Clown
15. The Alligator Tree
16. McKhoul the Ghoul
17. The Owl Man
18. The Octopus Tree
19. The Buffalo Tree
20. Chief Justice Kronox
21. Senator Gospelle
22. The Amunggus
23. Mrs. Steel's 1st Grade Class
24. Ace Stonebox

This symbol authenticates that this book was written by a person, or persons who have had, or may still have a debilitating illness, and who now write as a way to heal and encourage others.

9 781973 739401